Gabrielle Walker

My Burden to Bear

THE ULTIMATE PARABLE OF THE BIBLE

Take a closer look and discover how deep God's grace can go.

Copy Rights © 2024 by Gabrielle Walker. All rights reserved. No portion of this publication may be reproduced, stored in a retrieval system, or transmitted in any format by any means, electronic, mechanical, photocopy, recording, scanning, or otherwise, without prior written consent from this book's copyright owner and publisher.

ISBN: 979-8-9928540-6-0

LCCN: 2025913903

Printed in the United States of America

While the author of this book has made every effort to provide accurate Internet addresses at the time of publication, the author/publisher does not assume any responsibility for errors or changes that occur after publication. In addition, the author/publisher has no control over and does not assume any responsibility for websites or their content.

Scripture translations as well as Greek and Hebrew word transliterations have been retrieved from Bible Hub, an internet resource providing extensive biblical information. https://biblehub.com/. Bible verses provided by The World English Bible a public domain. Specific references are located in the Notes section of this book.

CONTENTS

INTRODUCTION vii
- *The Call Begins* vii
- *Different Bible Versions.* viii
- *The Call Begins Continued...* x

Prelude- *Getting to know Jesus.* 13

CHAPTER ONE *Getting to Know Jesus* 15
- *Jesus's Life on Earth* 16
- *Jesus in the Old Testament* 19

CHAPTER TWO *The Gift of Grace* 24
- *From Saul to Paul* 24
- *Jonah's Story:* 25

Prelude: *The Ultimate Parable* 28
- *How is this Considered a Parable?* 47

Chapter Three *Clarity and the Importance of Jesus's Way into the World* 54
- *Jesus came from the seed of David.* 56
- *Jesus, God in the flesh?* 60
- *Son of the Most High* 61

CONCLUSION 71
- *Take A Step Closer to Jesus* 75

NOTES: 76

Introduction

Hello to you all!

I would like to thank everyone in advance for reading this book and pray that you allow the Holy Spirit to lead in this reading and go to our Father with any questions you may have during this experience.

Simply put, this book is constructed to encourage the reader to begin researching the topic that is presented. So many examples could have been provided in this book for the proclamation regarding God's grace and, Jesus's Deity; However, it will be more edifying for you to find some of this information on your own. So, as there is a good variety of evidence to correlate with the *Ultimate Parable,* you will soon know there is much more to unveil in your studies. I would like to jump right in and get started. I am not one to sugarcoat anything. However, I always do my best to treat my siblings in Christ and my neighbors as I would want in return. In this case, with honesty, gentleness, and respect. First, I will give a bit of a story on how discovering this Ultimate Parable came about.

The Call Begins

Towards the end of 2023, I felt that the Holy Spirit was prompting me to purchase a new Bible while studying the Word. The only version I had in my physical possession was the King James Version. I started researching the differences between each version of the Bible. It became very overwhelming, so I prayed for God to lead me to which version I should buy. He led me to the NRSV 1989 version, so I purchased it. As I read my new Bible, the wording throughout this version caught my attention. I am sure many can relate to this. This new curiosity about the difference in word choice led me to dive into the definitions of these words in their original languages. I will not spoil anything; however, this unknowingly began my path to discovering the burden God assigned me to bring to the body of Christ.

Different Bible Versions.

Before continuing the "how" of this book coming into formation, I would like to take a moment to give my thoughts on the many versions of the Bible. It is important to discuss so we may lay a foundation of trust in God's word.

Though many versions of the Bible exist, I assure you there is no need to fear being misled; you will find your way to the truth. God has allowed these different versions to be accessible for a reason. The Bible is not corrupted. No matter what version a person reads, God will guide you to the information you need to see Jesus's true nature and fulfill your assignments if you are rooted in Him. Whether through family, friends, strangers, or a divine encounter alone with Him, if you truly have a pure heart towards God while accepting His guidance for His will to be fulfilled, the information will find its way to you. Nothing is hidden or new under the sun. The world differs in views because we refuse to see God's Word for what He tells us it is. We create narratives that conform our iniquities into justifiable acts. We are not willing to lay down our biases. A lot of times, we accept things as truths sometimes due to an emotional attachment to the source. This attachment may be attributed to a specific person, or this information can soothe our insecurity. Either way, the avenue of obtaining these "truths" and why we accept them can lead us to place more trust in them than in God. We are all resources simply because God is the only source of all things, and His truth must be ours.

Another thing that can bring barriers to seeing the truth is that many of us are not as familiar with God's voice as we should be, creating open doors to deception. God speaks to us through His Word; we must cultivate our relationship with Him through meditation and prayer to gain clarity. For us to perceive what He is saying correctly, we must allow Him to lead our path so that we are a willing participant in the unfolding of His inevitable will, thereby relinquishing heavy burdens over to Him that we would otherwise have to face alone, but I digress.

If we turn our lives over to God, we cannot give any created thing, human, or circumstance credit for what is given to or held back from us. Our lives are in God's hands, not man. Many proclaim God makes no mistakes, right? If we genuinely believe this, it must apply in all areas of life. Even if everyone spoke one language and had access to one version of the Bible, there would still be thousands of interpretations due to personal bias, purpose, and lack or gain of spiritual sight. This is why we must submit to God and let Him lead us in our studies. When we align with God and His will, the path for our lives will flow as it should. This doesn't mean that it will be easy; however, we will begin to receive information from His Word and be led in what should be done with it to advance the body of Christ as we are never provided knowledge of God and the kingdom just for ourselves. It may result in us testifying to a friend, parent, child, stranger, or a group of individuals; just know whatever knowledge God reveals concerning His word is to be released, but back to the point.

Before I had this view towards the different Bible versions, I believed one version was better than the others (now I just prefer one over the other). I noticed that I would disdain others who did not accept the version I preferred or told me my version was incorrect, as I am sure some felt the same regarding me as well. Believing that the wording used in certain versions was inaccurate or manipulative meant that those versions were planted to make me see God incorrectly. This may have been an agenda for some, only God knows a man's heart. But having different views forced me to lean on the ultimate source for confirmation, Jesus. After doing so, I realized it was another form of division I refused to participate in. I was freed from the delusion that any man can have power over my destined relationship with God.

Plenty of resources can be referenced to translate the original text into the interpreted language for those who require less faith-based trust in the different Bible translations. We live in the age of information, and with just an internet connection and a phone, how much knowledge we obtain regarding this subject is up to us. Of course, the most critical part is that we place God in the center of our studies and release any preconceived notions so that we may discern His affirming and rebuking correctly during our research. Do not be intimidated and start small. Pray, open your Bible, and ask God to guide you on where to start. Something will stand out for you, and you should begin there. It may not happen right away as we do not know God's timing, but I can say that He is pleased when we seek to follow His will for us and put action behind creating an intimate relationship with Him. God may direct you towards a verse, chapter, or a full book in the Bible to study and build from that.

The Call Begins Continued...

As I stated earlier, I began studying the NRSV version, and certain words began to stick out to me. This caused me to start researching translations of Hebrew and Greek words. It was very fascinating. When I started to understand that the purpose of these studies was to gear me toward writing this book, I was honored, nervous, and honestly felt unworthy of such a responsibility. I would like to state that I am not above anyone or believe I possess this special bond with God that no one else could ever obtain. God called me, and I picked up my cross to witness His glorious name.

    I was having difficulty accepting that God wanted me to write this book. Once I started studying the Bible and was certain this book was a part of my calling, I immediately thought, "I need to enroll in a biblical studies institution so I can pile up proof and be taken seriously." Promptly after having that thought, in my spirit, I believe God rebuked me. I did not understand why at the time, but He was helping me lean more on Him and not on man. Of course, we know that God is all for expanding our knowledge, especially concerning His Word. However, I was not permitted to conduct this through world education at that time because of my ability to be conflicted with what Abba was saying to me and society.

    There have been times in my life where I have felt the need to overexplain myself due to past experiences of judgment and ridicule for simply speaking on an event that had taken place in my life. It is a heartbreaking thing to be vulnerable with someone, and they see your scars as an instruction manual or road map to how you can be manipulated or controlled.

I refused to tell my stories of life's difficulties for many years. The last thing I wanted was pity from anyone. Something hurts your soul when you tell someone that you care for an event in your life that makes you look weak or naïve in their eyes, and the perception of you changes instantly. You are no longer as intelligent or wise as they thought you were. The judgment oozes out of them sometimes without them even having to say a word; it is all in their eyes. This would lead to a desire for me to redeem myself. So, I would overexplain and provide as many details as possible. It would start with me trying to deepen my connection with a loved one, then turn into me pleading a case.

But those stories are not for today; the point of me stating this is to testify that God brought me out of that desire and into the realization that only His opinion of me matters. Though I did not attend any Seminary or Biblical studies program before authoring this book, I believe God has supplied me with everything needed to complete this task. I do ask for your patience with me in that regard.

As I continued moving forward with the process of this book, I remained somewhat apprehensive. I was passionate about getting to know God intimately and was horrified at going against His will.

When God first confirmed the message of this book, I experienced attacks from the enemy and self-doubt that would confuse me. During this period in time I was weak in my faith simply because I did not fully submit myself to God; at this point in my life, I was still leading on my own understanding more than trusting Him. To ease these events, I sought shelter under Him and prayer saved me.

"Abba, I ask that you provide me with peace of mind and comfort in knowing I am always within your will concerning this. I ask that you correct any misinformation brought about by me or anyone else so that I may have no fear and no distortion of the message you gave me. As quickly as the enemy comes to steal my seed, I ask that you confirm that it has been planted in good soil. In Jesus name I pray, Amen."

This prayer was not worded the same every time, but it was sincere each moment I came to His feet for clarity.

After that, every thought of doubt that crept up was quickly wiped away and replaced with proof from the Scriptures for the original message God had given me, providing me peace to continue my studies and reading His Word. There were still moments of doubt that would come here and there, but God revealed the tools He had already equipped me with and taught me how to use them. With prayer, community, and meditating on His Word, I allowed myself to be caught if I fell.

I am not an expert in Theology nor am I a linguist regarding the Greek or Hebrew languages. However, I believe that God has provided me with enough information to bring forth the data displayed here with confidence.

Some may refuse to acknowledge this book in a weighty manner due to my level of education regarding biblical studies, while I pray that does not happen, if indeed it does, I am fine with it. I have followed the guidelines God has laid out for me. One thing that cannot be refuted is that all the claims in this book are easily accessible to everyone, open for discussion and backed up with what I believe is compelling evidence. I may come across very absolute and passionate throughout this book; however, this in no way translates to me not staying open to continuing to study this topic and being open to hearing differing opinions on the matter. The ultimate one to confirm this information is not me but God. So, always keep your eyes on Him no matter what any human proclaims; ask for confirmation from God and verification through His Word.

Prelude- *Getting to know Jesus.*

Jesus was sent to earth to be the ultimate atonement that would reconcile us back to the Father after Adam and Eve sinned. Genesis 3:12-15,

12 The man said, "The woman whom you gave to be with me, she gave me fruit from the tree, and I ate it."
13 Yahweh God said to the woman, "What have you done?"
The woman said, "The serpent deceived me, and I ate."
14 Yahweh God said to the serpent,
"Because you have done this,
  you are cursed above all livestock,
  and above every animal of the field.
You shall go on your belly
  and you shall eat dust all the days of your life.
15 I will put hostility between you and the woman,
  and between your offspring and her offspring.
He will bruise your head,
and you will bruise his heel."

Most of us know that the woman's seed, spoken of in Genesis 3 verse fifteen, refers to Jesus. We were given signs in scripture to point us to this conclusion.

One of the most well-known signs of the coming of Jesus was from the prophet Isaiah, 7:14

Therefore the Lord himself will give you a sign. Behold, the virgin will conceive, and bear a son, and shall call his name Immanuel."

Continuing with the prophet Isaiah, let us review more information regarding the coming of Jesus. This leads us into Chapter 1 of the book.

Chapter One

Getting to Know Jesus

In the book of Isaiah, we are given signs of how we will recognize the coming messiah. Although God informed us that the coming King would be of royalty, He also said that He would be "The Suffering Servant." Isaiah Chapters 52-53

I ask that you take a moment to read these scriptures before continuing.

This is a powerful scripture that can invoke a multitude of emotions. The best ones for me are gratefulness and feeling God's love for us through these words explaining the suffering that will take place to redeem humanity. I pray you take a minute to meditate and soak in this portion of Scripture and give thanksgiving and glory to God.

From reading the Scriptures regarding the suffering servant prophesied in the Old Testament, the King to come would not and did not present Himself in the ways humans would consider royal. Let us review some things we know regarding Jesus's life on earth.

Jesus's Life on Earth

Jesus's mother and father were told by many that He was anything but ordinary prior to and shortly after His birth; however, this theme was not continuously portrayed to us throughout His teen and early adult years. Many aspects of His life were seemingly ordinary. His mother and father were not of much notoriety; although Joseph was of the line of David, the span between Joseph's and David's lives was about one thousand years apart. Jesus's family was not wealthy; Joseph was a carpenter. Our Savior's human existence was a very humble one.

In the gospel of Luke, we are told that Jesus (at the age of twelve) was found in a Temple listening and asking questions to the teachers, and they all were amazed at His comprehension and answers to what was being discussed; however, this most likely wouldn't give much insight or enough clarity for Jesus to be recognized as the Messiah at this point in time. The teachers may have believed He was just advanced in understanding Biblical principles. Jesus did not start His ministry until 30, and His hometown of Nazareth did not recognize His true nature then.

Mark 6:1-6

He went out from there. He came into his own country, and his disciples followed him. ² When the Sabbath had come, he began to teach in the synagogue, and many hearing him were astonished, saying, "Where did this man get these things?" and, "What is the wisdom that is given to this man, that such mighty works come about by his hands? ³ Isn't this the carpenter, the son of Mary and brother of James, Joses, Judah, and Simon? Aren't his sisters here with us?" So they were offended at him.

⁴ Jesus said to them, "A prophet is not without honor, except in his own country, and among his own relatives, and in his own house." ⁵ He could do no mighty work there, except that he laid his hands on a few sick people and healed them. ⁶ He marveled because of their unbelief.

Though Jesus came across as common to many around Him prior to beginning His ministry, there are some questions as to why not one person would deem Him to be divine simply due to His virgin birth. Even those who are spiritually blind would have to take into consideration that Jesus was unique to some extent (prior to performing miracles) due to Him being born from a virgin.
Looking at the prophet Isaiah's words again in Chapter 7:14, we must seek some form of clarity to connect why no one deemed Jesus as divine due to His virgin birth.

The scripture states that a virgin will conceive and bear a son. The next question I would ask is, why did God choose to send Jesus to earth through a virgin?
I do not believe it is to make a spectacle of Jesus's arrival into the world due to this going against the humble pattern of His life. Those who were able to see Jesus's Holy nature before His ministry were provided that privilege by God.
We can also say that Jesus was not born of a virgin to ensure that He would not inherit the sins of His parents because of Ezekiel 18:20.

"The soul who sins, he shall die. The son shall not bear the iniquity of the father, neither shall the father bear the iniquity of the son. The righteousness of the righteous shall be on him, and the wickedness of the wicked shall be on him."

I am about to declare something that will make many of us uncomfortable, confused, shocked, and even downright angry. But this message has been told before.
However, in this case, this revelation is truly that. Something that has always been the truth but has just been revealed in a way for us that is

hopefully easier to comprehend.

Before we become too attached to our feelings, let us put them aside and try to think logically when we read the following statement.

Jesus Christ was not born of a virgin.

I assure you this is nothing personal or meant to offend anyone; it is simply the truth.

I was not struggling with the ins and outs of how a virgin birth was possible, and it did not compromise my faith. I was perfectly fine with not having a complete understanding of this miracle. However, when I posed the question of the virgin birth to God after reading the new Bible He led me to purchase; this is what was given to me.

The more The Holy Spirit led me, the more I realized that this was my burden. This is what God has called me to proclaim. I will do as He has commanded me until my dying breath because my obedience is to Him and not man.

 I encourage everyone to do their research as the Holy Spirit leads. Self-seeking is extremely dangerous and causes confusion and bias to be placed unnecessarily. When we are led to dive deeper into the truths of the Scriptures by God, it is simply to advance the kingdom. It is not to win an argument or seize it as an opportunity to showcase our intellectual capacity.

 This book intends to clarify the Deity of Christ Jesus, free us from religious strongholds, and show God's true love and grace. It also aims to spark you to start or continue your journey of getting to know our creator better. God takes pleasure in us diligently seeking Him within His Word and throughout every aspect of our lives.

I know this is a sensitive subject for many of us, and it will be difficult for some to be open to this even being possible. But I encourage you to seek God throughout your reading He will provide you with His peace regarding this.

So, let's begin.

Jesus in the Old Testament

I will give a few examples of Jesus in the Old Testament.
This data sets a foundation for the intricate information that will follow later. However, it will not be extensive.
In this Bible verse, the slave girl Hagar has run away due to the harsh treatment of Abram's wife, Sarai. She is pregnant with Abram's child after being told to have intercourse with him to conceive due to Sarai being barren. The Angel of the Lord (Jesus) comes to her.
When reading Genesis 16:7-12, God comes to Hagar and comforts her. Letting her know she will bear a son; she is to name him Ishmael. The Lord tells her about the boy's life and that he will have many offspring.

"Yahweh's angel found her by a fountain of water in the wilderness, by the fountain on the way to Shur. ⁸ He said, "Hagar, Sarai's servant, where did you come from? Where are you going?"

She said, "I am fleeing from the face of my mistress Sarai."

⁹ Yahweh's angel said to her, "Return to your mistress, and submit yourself under her hands." ¹⁰ Yahweh's angel said to her, "I will greatly multiply your offspring, that they will not be counted for multitude." ¹¹ Yahweh's angel said to her, "Behold, you are with child, and will bear a son. You shall call his name Ishmael, because Yahweh has heard your affliction. ¹² He will be like a wild donkey among men. His hand will be against every man, and every man's hand against him. He will live opposed to all of his brothers."

Continuing to Genesis 16:13, Hagar calls the one she spoke to "The God who sees."

"She called the name of Yahweh who spoke to her, "You are a God who sees," for she said, "Have I even stayed alive after seeing him?"

The Hebrew transliteration Yahweh is used in this thirteenth verse, The verse states that the one who came to Hagar, "The Angel of the Lord" is Yahweh. Hagar refers to Him as the God who sees and is in awe that she is still alive after seeing God with her own eyes in a physical form.

In Genesis Chapter 18, Abraham sees the Lord. In verse one this is stated, ***"Yahweh appeared to him by the oaks of Mamre, as he sat in the tent door in the heat of the day."***

Next, in verse two, Abraham is visited by three men, one of whom he bow's down to, and we are told Abraham addresses Him as Lord.
If we read Genesis 18:2-3 (When Abraham bow's down to a man and calls Him Lord), it correlates with John 8:56 (when Jesus spoke to the Jews and said Abraham rejoiced to see His day.).

Genesis 18:2-3,

"He lifted up his eyes and looked, and saw that three men stood near him. When he saw them, he ran to meet them from the tent door, and bowed himself to the earth, ³ *and said, "My lord, if now I have found favor in your sight, please don't go away from your servant.".*

John 8:56,

"Your father Abraham rejoiced to see my day. He saw it and was glad."

Later in Genesis 18:20-21, this is said,

"Yahweh said, "Because the cry of Sodom and Gomorrah is great, and because their sin is very grievous, ²¹ *I will go down now, and see whether their deeds are as bad as the reports which have come to me. If not, I will know."*

When we get to Genesis 19, the destruction of Sodom and Gomorrah is being described. Verse 24 states, ***"Then Yahweh rained on Sodom***

and Gomorrah sulfur and fire from Yahweh out of the sky."

Your bible translation may say "The Lord" instead of Yahweh however, both times this word is used in verse twenty-four, it translates to Yahweh in Hebrew. When reading this verse, it may seem as though the phrasing can be attributed to just the use of illeism. However, we have already established that in Genesis 18:20-21, Yahweh tells Abraham that He will go to Sodom and Gomorrah. We know that there are not two Gods, right? So, stating that Jesus is the angel of the Lord and the **Yahweh** that is physically in Sodom and Gomorrah is more than understandable especially after reviewing the correlation between John 8:56 and Genesis 18:2-3. The connection between these scriptures gives me no doubt that Jesus is God in the flesh. Hagar was able to live after stating she saw God. She was not corrected by the Angel of the Lord so we are safe with interpreting this as just what it said, she saw God.

Please keep an open heart while reading this book and I ask that you fully submit yourself to the word of God and not mine so that true revelation can be had. To receive revelation from God, we must realize that our minds can only comprehend to a certain point. This is why when God gives us revelation, it is a gift. Who would you rather be—someone who recites the entire Bible or receives the true meaning behind the Scriptures? The second option can only come if God allows it. Relying solely on the wisdom of man will lead us astray every time.

For this last example, I will provide a text from the Old and New Testaments that correlate.

Mark 14:60-62, *"The high priest stood up in the middle, and asked Jesus, "Have you no answer? What is it which these testify against you?" ⁶¹ But he stayed quiet, and answered nothing. Again the high priest asked him, "Are you the Christ, the Son of the Blessed?*

⁶² Jesus said, "I am. You will see the Son of Man sitting at the right hand of Power, and coming with the clouds of the sky."

Daniel 7:13-14, *"I saw in the night visions, and behold, there came with the clouds of the sky one like a son of man, and he came even to the Ancient of Days, and they brought him near before him. ¹⁴ Dominion was given him, and glory, and a kingdom, that all the peoples, nations, and languages should serve him. His dominion is an everlasting dominion, which will not pass away, and his kingdom one that will not be destroyed."*

We know that we are only to give glory and serve God. In Mark 14:60–62, Jesus claims to be the Son of Man spoken of in Daniel 7:13-14.

Many try to dispute that Jesus never proclaimed that He is God due to Him not wording it exactly how they desired to hear it. The way He brings forth this information should be a completely acceptable form of communicating this revelation, seeing as though Jesus is well-known for using parables to reveal the truth.

Though this may anger some, I pray that it piques some interest in all of us to continue looking further into seeing Jesus in the Old Testament, as there are several more examples of this throughout it. It is quite amazing when it is revealed to you repeatedly in the Bible. Do your studies with God as your solidifier. If this portion of the book has captured your interest, I would recommend *The Deity of Jesus Christ in the Old and New Testaments* (Gurbikian, 2011).

There comes a time when we are all called to be diligent in our relationship with God so that we may come to know Him properly. Pray to our Father that He gives you a heart to know Him more, and He will surely provide that to you.

God can give all of us revelation; if that occurs, we are to proclaim it to the body of Christ so that we may be strengthened. It is evangelizing; we are all important to the church's building. Some may be provided more information regarding the revelation of the Bible than others; however, none will have revelation to all the meanings for every scripture in God's Word. We are to study the scriptures with integrity, truth, and an open heart to not place our own bias on the Word of God. The revelations we begin to have while reading scripture are deemed fruitful by producing evidence of God's glory, deity, and will for humanity.

We must invite God into everything we do to accomplish the tasks He has for us. There is always a purpose behind everything God allows us to see. This section of the book not only proclaims Jesus as Lord but aims to open your mind so that you may grasp the concept of how and why Jesus could not have been born of a virgin.

Chapter Two

The Gift of Grace
From Saul to Paul

As stated in Ephesians 2:8-9, grace is a gift that God can give to all of us. It is not something that can be earned.

In the Bible, we see several examples of God providing grace. For many, one of the most notable is the grace and mercy God bestowed upon Saint Paul, formerly Saul. He was a Pharisee (a religious leader in the Jewish community who strictly followed their laws and customs) and was actively pursuing the persecution of people of the Way. Jesus stops Saul on his way to Damascus and before this chapter ends in the book of Acts, Paul is proclaiming Jesus's name in the synagogues!
Whether you know Paul's story or are unfamiliar with it, I recommend

reading Acts chapter 9; it is a great reminder of God's just and forgiving nature.

Reading about the way Paul's conversion from Judaism to The Way formed due to his experience of God's rebuke, mercy, and correction; is a fitting example of how God can reach us in ways we do not realize we need. Paul believed that he was doing the work of God by defending his religion via punishing those who he deemed as not revering God correctly. This gift of grace made Paul a target for other Jewish leaders but overall, Paul received what I believe he was seeking the most which was honoring God in the way He desires. By Paul relinquishing his pride he was able to humbly accept God's grace.

Another beautiful gift of grace in the Bible is that of Jonah.
One thing I enjoy regarding Jonah's gift of grace is that it typically is not viewed as such in the way I will expound upon.

Jonah struggled with something a lot of us have or will encounter, and that is thinking we can predict what God will do and why He does it. As Isaiah 55:7-9 states God's thoughts are not our thoughts and our ways are not His either.

Jonah's Story:

Jonah was told to deliver a message of the coming of God's wrath upon the people of Nineveh due to their wickedness. However, Jonah did not see the point in him going, as he believed that God would forgive them regardless. He tried to escape God's presence and got on a boat to Tarshish. Short story shorter, God caused a great wind upon the sea, and Jonah ends up being thrown overboard because it is discovered that he is the cause of the great wind. God had a great fish that He prepared, swallowed Jonah, and he was in the fish's belly for three days and three nights. While in the belly of the fish, Jonah prayed to the Lord, giving thanks and vowing to sacrifice to Him. God cast Jonah out of the fish and told him again to go to Nineveh and proclaim the warning message, and Jonah did. After hearing the message, the people of Nineveh repented, fasted, and put on sackcloth. When God saw what the people did, he provided grace and mercy upon them.

This upset Jonah, and he spoke to God, saying.

Jonah 4:2

"So he prayed to the Lord, ***and said, "Ah,*** Lord, ***was not this what I said when I was still in my country? Therefore I fled previously to Tarshish; for I know that You are a gracious and merciful God, slow to anger and abundant in lovingkindness, One who relents from doing harm."***

Jonah does not understand the why of God's actions regarding this situation and is angered that the Lord did not bring His wrath upon the people of Nineveh. Jonah is speaking to God, saying he knows He is slow to anger and has great kindness, while in the same breath, being angered that God did not unleash his wrath on the people of Nineveh. The people of Nineveh humbled themselves; God is willing to hear a sincerely humble heart.

He still has much growing to do; let us be honest, Jonah believed it was possible to flee from God's presence, yet he is a prophet. We could see this as a lack of knowledge, but it is the opposite. Jonah has chosen a self-imposed delusion over the truth. Why? Because this delusion allows him to maintain a sense of comfort in the midst of his disobedience towards God. We all have or will do this at some point in our lives. We will face a situation that feels too large for us to address. Instead of relinquishing these overwhelming thoughts to God so He may walk us through them, we suppress them and pretend the situation does not exist or is not our issue anymore. We find ways to work around it, so our discomfort is put to ease, thus creating self-imposed delusion.

Jonah was upset that God did not punish Nineveh because he wanted a particular reward for his work, everything he did to make it to Nineveh. He repented for his disobedience and vowed to sacrifice for God. He finally headed to Nineveh to deliver the message, and the journey was not easy. He endured a lot and believed that he redeemed himself in the eyes of God. When God gave His final judgment to spare the people of Nineveh, Jonah felt his obedience was not rewarded in the way he saw fit, which, in this case, he thought the reward for his sacrifice would equate to the destruction of wicked people. Secondly, Jonah viewed the people of Nineveh as too far gone for redemption and disdained their wicked ways. Jonah saw himself as better than the people of Nineveh. We, as humans, will never possess the level of grace and compassion that God provides us. We should never expect to receive something in return just because we have sacrificed to the Lord or anyone. Sacrifice should stem from reverence for our God and love for one another.

Later, while Jonah was resting, God provided a bush for him to have shade from the sun. Jonah was happy, but God appointed a worm to attack the bush the next day, which withered. Then God let the sun beat down on Jonah. Exhausted from the heat, Jonah states that it is better for him to die than live in chapter 4, verse eight.

In verses nine to eleven, God asks Jonah if it is right that he is angry about the plant being destroyed and Jonah replies that it is right for him to be angry even enough to die.

God then says to Jonah that he has pity for a plant that he did not nurture and appeared in one night and then perished in one night. God asks Jonah if He should not have pity on Nineveh a large city that has over one hundred and twenty thousand people that do not know how to discern their right hand from their left?

Jonah's care for the plant was merely due to what it provided for him—shade from the heat, so it was worth living by its works. This is his viewpoint regarding the people of Nineveh; they did not provide anything of good substance to God in Jonah's eyes, so even though he knows God's nature of forgiveness, Jonah did not approve of their wickedness going unpunished.

God's care for the people of Nineveh stems from His love for us. We get confused thinking God just wants us to obey Him because He is God; no, God wants us to obey Him because it will prosper us. Our God loves us so much that He will not stand for those who chose blatant disobedience of His word, trying to coerce or encourage those who are in disobedience, not from willful rebellion but ignorance. God is showing the steadfast love for His children, a character trait that Jonah believed he was so knowledgeable of. God is telling Jonah that He protects the fools of the world. The people of Nineveh did not have discernment, and it was not their hearts that were impure; it was their ways. When they were corrected, their true nature was tested, and they passed. We all must be tested; it does not matter whether we believe we know the outcome. It is part of our free will to obey God or refuse, and He provided this choice to us.

The gift of grace here is for the people of Nineveh and Jonah. Not that God provided a fish for him to safely dwell in for three days (although that is part of it), but the grace God is providing Jonah during his walk of getting to know his Lord better.

God was so patient with Jonah because He knew his heart. The ending of this book does not shed light on whether Jonah has learned to stop thinking he can predict God's ways and His reasoning for them; however, I enjoy the inconclusive ending as it represents a true season of growing in a relationship with God. One that does not end with us coming to full understanding but still willing to follow the path our Father is providing for us. This is an example of God preparing His children for things ahead. Sometimes, we do not understand the lesson God is trying to teach us right away, but later, we will see why it was so important for us to learn it.

There are many examples of God giving grace to people in the Bible. Now I will show one last example of this gift that many do not view as such.

I like to refer to this gift of grace as **"The Ultimate Parable."**

I encourage you to take your time and digest the information in this section of the book. I ask that you do not jump to any conclusions and remain curious while seeking the Lord.

Prelude: *The Ultimate Parable*

In Matthew chapter 1, we are given the lineage of Jesus, son of David,

son of Abraham. In verse sixteen, we are told, "And Jacob begets Joseph, the husband of Mary, whom Jesus was born.
We must dig deep to expand our minds and grasp what is happening in this chapter alone. The Bible reiterates Joseph being of the line of David in various sections.
Due to many of us not studying the Bible for ourselves, we have overlooked simple things that tell us that Joseph is the father of Jesus. That last sentence may have struck a nerve, but again, I implore you to stay with me until the end.

Matthew Chapter 1 verse eighteen,

"Now the birth of Jesus Christ was like this: After his mother, Mary, was engaged to Joseph, before they came together, she was found pregnant by the Holy Spirit."

When this eighteenth verse in Matthew Chapter 1 states that Mary was engaged or pledged to Joseph, this means they are legally promising each one to the other. As we continue to read this verse, it states, "before they came together, she was found pregnant, by the Holy Spirit."
Now, context matters so let us put the pieces together therefore bringing clarity to the statement I just made regarding Joseph being Jesus's father.

The transliterated Greek word for *"came together"* in this verse is **sunerchomai,** which means (to come together, to accompany cohabitate, or to assemble).

We are told that Joseph and Mary are engaged, but before they "came together," she was found pregnant. Most of us see this coming together as a euphemism for sexual intercourse, bringing our conclusion of this verse to mean that Mary and Joseph were engaged but before they had sexual relations with one another, Mary was found pregnant.
Keeping context at the forefront, and after reviewing the definition of the transliterated Greek word, for *came together,* I believe the meaning of this equates to Joseph and Mary not yet living together and or, having their marriage ceremony at the time she was found to be pregnant. The

word cohabitation does not always mean the people involved are living together and simultaneously having sexual relations for a fact; but it does *always* equate to the fact that the persons cohabitating are living together and are not legally married. There are bible versions that say, "before they were married" or "before they lived together" which implies that there is no need to fear a grammatical error when replacing one phrase with the other. This word, **sunerchomai,** is used over twenty-five times in the New Testament and has no sexual implications in any other verse except in Matthew 1:18.

Finally, the end of this verse says, "by the Holy Spirit."

I believe this does not refer to the Holy Spirit impregnating her with the vessel; this is stating the role that Holy Spirit played in Jesus entering the womb.

So, let us put this whole verse into the context that is being tested of Joesph being Jesus's father.

Mary and Joseph are betrothed, we would say engaged, but during biblical times, couple's positions in the betrothal stage are taken as seriously as a husband and wife during this time; however, the wedding and consummation of the official marriage would take place farther down the line.

Mary was pregnant before she and Joseph were officially married via a ceremony, and Holy Spirit has placed Jesus into the vessel they have created. Now, why am I saying was placed into the vessel? This is where chapter one's information is critical to comprehend. We know that Jesus existed before the beginning of time. Therefore, it is impossible for Mary and Holy Spirit to have "created" Jesus. He was simply placed in a human vessel produced by Mary and Joseph to be born into the world.

Now, we will review verse nineteen in Matthew Chapter 1.

"Joseph, her husband, being a righteous man, and not willing to make her a public example, intended to put her away secretly."

The first part of this verse refers to Joseph as Mary's husband, even though a wedding has not occurred yet. It is worded this way due to how seriously the betrothal stage is taken in Jewish customs.

This verse states that Joseph was a righteous being unwilling to make her a public example, so he intended to put her away secretly.

With doing our best to stay in context while identifying the relevance of each verse to the other, this opens the door to view this portion of scripture naming Joseph as righteous and unwilling to publicly expose Mary stemming from his knowing that she did not have relations with another man. Let me explain.

If Joseph genuinely believed that another man impregnated Mary, the law states that her and the man she laid with would be stoned to death had she broken the covenant she made with Joseph; thereby creating an environment that paints Joseph as willingly aiding in Mary breaking this law by trying to conceal Mary's actions. We will review these laws in the book of Deuteronomy soon.

At the end of verse nineteen, Joesph is thinking of secretly sending Mary away to avoid public humiliation. The implication that most of us conclude when reading this is that Joseph is seeking to divorce Mary.

Notably when seeing the phrase "send her away" its common meaning is pertaining to a husband seeking to divorce his wife. However, it can also mean just simply sending someone away. The Greek transliterated word in this verse for "send her away" is ***apoluó***. This word can be used in a reflexive manner meaning when Joseph planned to send her away, this decision was basically a knee jerk reaction/option to resolve the problem at hand by sending her away in a literal sense and not in a repudiate way.

Continuing on with keeping the context going, again, Joseph "sending Mary away" can imply that he is thinking of doing just that, sending her away so that she will not be seen while she is pregnant therefore saving her from public disgrace.

As stated earlier, if Joseph believed that Mary is pregnant with another man's child during their betrothal, when this knowledge is made public, she will be at risk for death by stoning. It seems a bit peculiar that Joseph would have the understanding that Mary's life is at risk, yet the only concern stated in the verse is directed at her dishonor and not her life.

In the Book of Deuteronomy, laws concerning sex and marriage.

Deuteronomy 22:23-27

"If there is a young lady who is a virgin pledged to be married to a husband, and a man finds her in the city, and lies with her, ²⁴ then you shall bring them both out to the gate of that city, and you shall stone them to death with stones; the lady, because she didn't cry, being in the city; and the man, because he has humbled his neighbor's wife. So you shall remove the evil from among you. ²⁵ But if the man finds the lady who is pledged to be married in the field, and the man forces her and lies with her, then only the man who lay with her shall die; ²⁶ but to the lady you shall do nothing. There is in the lady no sin worthy of death; for as when a man rises against his neighbor and kills him, even so is this matter; ²⁷ for he found her in the field, the pledged to be married lady cried, and there was no one to save her."

Verse twenty-three and twenty-four gives provision over if a betrothed (engaged) woman meets a man and lays with him. The law states that they both shall be stoned to death.

These are laws Moses gave from God. Implying that Joseph wanted to go against God's law by trying to conceal Mary breaking her covenant with him is a dangerous accusation. This also implies that Joseph is either willing to lie to the witnesses that would need to be present to end the betrothal or tell the truth and possibly hope that they will keep the reason for the ending of the betrothal a secret so Mary will not face punishment for her actions.

That would put Joseph in an unrighteous position as well as the witnesses. Ultimately, keeping Mary's "supposed" infidelity a secret while simultaneously granting a divorce for Joseph, ignores the Law that God put into place for if this specific event ever were to occur.

I would also like to draw our attention to the fact that no law in this chapter pertains to the situation that Mary and Joseph found themselves in. They are betrothed to each other and have had relations before the wedding ceremony. This is why Joseph is more concerned regarding Mary potentially suffering public disgrace and shame rather than stoning/punishment.

We can all agree that a betrothed couple consummating their marriage before the ceremony has taken place was not an acceptable practice, however, when referring to the laws Moses gave from God regarding sexual relations, an event of this nature is not documented, therefore when we read that Joseph is concerned with Mary's reputation and not her life being in danger, it is completely understandable and concludes that Joseph can be considered a righteous man due to this reasoning.

Now let us put all of Matthew 1:18-19 into full context.

Mary and Joseph are betrothed, However, before their wedding ceremony Mary is discovered to be pregnant. Now we have discussed how Jesus has always been in existence so with this verse mentioning the Holy Spirit, it is in reference to Jesus being placed in the vessel not Him being created. Joseph is not aware that the child Mary is carrying has a divine purpose, he just knows that Mary is going to have a baby.

Joseph did not want Mary to be disgraced so he thought about sending her away secretly so this would not occur. We reviewed how Joseph sending Mary away can mean he is thinking of doing just that, sending her away and not requesting a divorce.

This conclusion validates Joseph being a righteous man. By him not believing that Mary committed adultery, we can safely say that Joseph is not trying to circumvent Gods law and is simply trying to protect Mary from public humiliation when the time comes for their wedding ceremony. There is no law outlining the consequences pertaining to a betrothed couple having relations before their ceremony and this is why Joseph is concerned with Mary's dishonor rather than her being at risk for death by stoning.

Now, we will continue diving into Matthew Chapter 1:20-21

"But when he thought about these things, behold, an angel of the Lord appeared to him in a dream, saying, "Joseph, son of David, don't be afraid to take to yourself Mary as your wife, for that which

is conceived in her is of the Holy Spirit. ²¹ She shall give birth to a son. You shall name him Jesus, for it is he who shall save his people from their sins."

While Joseph is thinking about sending Mary away to avoid public disgrace, an angel comes to him in a dream and tells Joseph that he does not have to worry and to still take Mary as his wife because the child in her is from the Holy Spirit and has a great purpose.

Now let us continue with our context and dissect what the angel is *not* telling Joseph to do, which is divorce Mary. The angel tells him not to be afraid to take Mary as his wife, these are two vastly different things. If Joseph's meaning behind the term "send her away" was intended to proceed with a divorce, I would believe that the angel would have addressed this. The angel mentions nothing about seeking divorce but taking Mary as his wife, how would this occur? At a wedding ceremony. With the angel telling Joseph not to be afraid to take Mary as his wife, this leaves space for us to stay within the context that we have been concluding, which is that Joseph is trying to steer clear of a public ceremony to avoid Mary's shame and not the marriage altogether. Again, this section shines light on Joseph's true concern, which was Mary's public disgrace. Why would Mary be at risk for public disgrace? Because just as it said in Matthew 1 verse eighteen, she was pregnant before her and Joseph's wedding ceremony. As in those days, a betrothal could last as long as 1 year. It seems highly possible that Mary would be discovered to be pregnant before their ceremony. Weddings typically lasted five to seven days; there would be no way to hide her pregnancy for that period without Joseph and Mary revealing the child to someone.

If you would like more information about the betrothal stage, I would recommend *Manners and Customs of the Bible-A Complete Guide to The Origin and Significance of Our Time-Honoured Biblical-* (Freeman, 1972).

Continuing with verse twenty and twenty-one, The angel tells Joseph what is conceived in her is of the Holy Spirit and the child's purpose to save their people from their sins.

Of course, we know that Jesus is Holy so in my interpretation, this is what qualifies the vessel to be deemed as such. Jesus is dwelling in the vessel thereby it is made Holy.

Matthew Chapter 1 Verse 22-23

"Now all this has happened that it might be fulfilled which was spoken by the Lord through the prophet, saying,
²³ "Behold, the virgin shall be with child,
  and shall give birth to a son.
They shall call his name Immanuel,"
  which is, being interpreted, "God with us."

The word virgin in verse twenty-three is the Greek word **Parthenos,** meaning maiden, virgin, or referring to an unmarried woman.

This brings me to my next point. There is a book called the Septuagint or the LXX that I am sure many of you are familiar with. It is an early translation of the Old Testament from Hebrew to Greek, dating back to the third century. In Genesis 34:1-4 Dinah, daughter of Jacob and Leah has just been sexually assaulted, and her assailant (Shechem, son of Hamor the Hivite), who is a prince, asked his father to retrieve Dinah as his wife. In verse four this is stated,

⁴ Shechem spoke to his father, Hamor, saying, "Get me this young lady as a wife."

The transliterated Greek word **Parthenos** in the Septuagint is used to describe Leah (*young lady*) after her assault. She is not a virgin anymore; however, she *is* unmarried. So, interpreting this verse as Shechem asking his father to retrieve Dinah and him referring to her as an unmarried woman or young woman to become his wife is more plausible than us comprehending this verse as Shechem asking his father to retrieve Dinah a virgin, to become his wife after he has defiled her. Leaving credible room to say that the word Parthenos does not always equate to a virgin.

Now, as we just reviewed the Greek meaning of the transliterated word for virgin in Genesis 34:4, we will review the word used for virgin in Isaiah 7:14 in the Hebrew language which is transliterated as **"*almah*,"** which means a virgin, and an unmarried woman. The word almah can be used to describe a virgin who is unmarried, but that is usually implied when speaking of a young woman. When seeing the word almah, it does not indicate that the woman is a virgin as a fact, it could be about an unmarried woman, just as ***Parthenos*** can.

The word almah is used in different contexts that show that while it is understandable to assume a woman being called almah is a virgin, it does not explicitly refer to a woman's sexual history or her unequivocally being a virgin. This word has multiple implications. As we already discussed, virgin and unmarried women but also young maidens. Referring to Isaiah 7:14, some scholars believe that this is a dual prophecy, meaning it was fulfilled in Isaiah's time and, of course, about Jesus's arrival into the world in the gospel of Matthew.

The first fulfillment of the prophecy is seen in the following verse. Isaiah 8:3-4, *"I went to the prophetess, and she conceived, and bore a son. Then Yahweh said to me, "Call his name 'Maher Shalal Hash Baz.' ⁴ For before the child knows how to say, 'My father' and 'My mother,' the riches of Damascus and the plunder of Samaria will be carried away by the king of Assyria."*

After reviewing Isaiah 8:3-4 the best definition for the word almah in Chapter 7:14 which can correctly identify this as referring to Isaiah's wife can only be as a young woman. We cannot say she is unmarried or that she is a virgin because the verse is speaking of Isaiah and his wife conceiving their second child. This is an example of the word "almah" not having any sexual undertone.

One more example can be found in Exodus 2:8. When the Pharaoh's daughter finds Moses, Moses' sister asks her if she can call the Hebrew woman to nurse Moses.

"Pharaoh's daughter said to her, "Go."
The young woman went and called the child's mother."

The word almah is used when Moses's sister is called young woman. Given the context of this Scripture, it is safe to say the use of the word almah in this verse is describing a young woman, showing the use of this word is not explicitly aimed to identify a woman's sexual history yet again. With all we just reviewed regarding the words **Parthenos** and ***almah***, logic is left for Mary to be deemed the almah, fulfilling the prophecy in Isaiah 7:14 without needing to be a virgin. How? We know that Mary is a young woman, an adjective she can identify as that still qualifies her to be considered an almah and she is also technically unmarried.

(Please see the *Notes* section of this book to review the article *"Chapter 18E-The Virgin Misconception Myth"* from JewsforJudaism.org and do your research to conclude regarding this translation).

Now, we can jump back into Matthew 1: 24-25.

Translation Greek to English: ***"Having been awoken then Joseph from the sleep, he did as had commanded him the angel of the Lord, and received the wife of him, <u>and not knew</u> her until that she had brought forth a son; and he called the name of Him Jesus."***

The word "and" in verse twenty-five were it states ***"<u>and not knew her until she had brought forth a son;</u>"*** is the Greek transliterated word ***kai***. This word can be translated into many conjunctions such as ***and, also, both, but, even, for,*** and a lot more terms. Several bible versions have the word "but" in place of the word "and" in this scripture leaving a clearer interpretation of what is taking place here. Stay with me as I connect these dots.

Reviewing the word "knew' also in verse twenty-five we can see that the Greek word for this is transliterated as ***ginosko***, which means to come to know, recognize, or perceive. This word has no sexual implications in its definition. While I do not disagree with the possibility that this word could be used to describe a viewpoint in which a woman has had sexual relations, I do not believe that is the intended definition in this scripture. The word "knew" in this verse is referencing to Joseph not coming to know Mary as his wife until after she gave birth to Jesus. Look at verses twenty-four and twenty-five again while keeping in mind of the Greek word ***kai*** that can be used as "and *or* but" with no conflict in grammar, and the word "knew" being used to convey its definition and not being utilized as a euphemism.

We can see that there is no discrepancy in stating that this information we are being told is simply stating that Joseph did as the angel commanded which was to take Mary as his wife, however this event did not occur until after Jesus was born. Again, when this twenty-fifth verse in Matthew chapter 1 says Joseph did not *"know"* Mary until she brought forth a Son (Jesus), it is referring to Joseph and Mary not *"coming together"* via their wedding ceremony until after Jesus was born. The angel told Joseph not to be afraid to take Mary as his wife; nothing regarding sexual intercourse was discussed during this interaction. So, us staying in the context, when the Scripture says, Joseph did as the angel of the Lord commanded and took Mary as his wife, but he did not know her until she had brought forth her firstborn Son, it is stating Joseph and Mary had their wedding as the angel commanded; however, he did not do so until after Jesus was born.

Further evidence in Luke Chapter 2:4–7 aligns with this context and interpretation, showing that Mary and Joseph did not get married until after Jesus was born.

"Joseph also went up from Galilee, out of the city of Nazareth, into Judea, to David's city, which is called Bethlehem, because he was of the house and family of David, ⁵ to enroll himself with Mary, who was pledged to be married to him as wife, being pregnant.

⁶ While they were there, the day had come for her to give birth. ⁷ She gave birth to her firstborn son. She wrapped him in bands of cloth and laid him in a feeding trough, because there was no room for them in the inn."

The fifth verse clearly stated that Mary and Joseph were still in the betrothal stage when Jesus was born, which correlated to Matthew 1:25 referring to Joseph taking Mary as his wife but not until after she gave birth to Jesus. Again, it is not referring to them not having sexual relations.

The Bible gives us the detail of Mary and Joseph still being engaged when they go to register, and while doing so, she gives birth to Jesus, for a reason. It is to correlate these two scriptures context and confirm what has been stated here. Let us read these two portions of scripture again keeping the context we are currently in.

Matthew 1:24-25

"Having been awoken then Joseph from the sleep, he did as had commanded him the angel of the Lord, and received the wife of him, "but" not "knew" her until that she had brought forth a son; and he called the name of Him Jesus."

Luke 2:2-7

"Joseph also went up from Galilee, out of the city of Nazareth, into Judea, to David's city, which is called Bethlehem, because he was of the house and family of David, ⁵ to enroll himself with Mary, who was pledged to be married to him as wife, being pregnant.

⁶ While they were there, the day had come for her to give birth. ⁷ She gave birth to her firstborn son. She wrapped him in bands of cloth and laid him in a feeding trough, because there was no room for them in the inn."

Mary and Joseph were in the betrothal stage when the angel came to Joseph. With this information, we can safely say that Joseph did not fulfill the angels command of taking Mary as his wife until after she gives birth to Jesus due to Luke 2:4-7. Again, we are given the detail that they are still engaged at the time of Jesus's birth for a reason. Having provided this information we are able to stay in the context that nothing sexual was discussed between Joseph and the angel and the focus was regarding the wedding ceremony.

I am reiterating my points often to hopefully convey the message I am bringing forth as clearly as possible.

When interpreting the Bible, verses cannot contradict one another. Reviewing the information, you will see that this interpretation does not contradict the scriptures we have reviewed. No words have been removed nor replaced; we are just looking deeper into the meaning behind them.

I pray this information is being taken in with an open mind and placed at our Father's feet for any clarification. Again, I implore you to read this book in its entirety before rushing to any judgment.

I encourage you to take a break here and read Matthew Chapter 1 with this information in mind. I believe you will see that the scriptures provide a detailed account of a groom trying to protect his bride from the judgement and cruelty of the world and not trying to release himself from his marriage obligation.

Now that we have broken down Matthew's account of Jesus's birth let us head over to Luke.

Luke Chapter 1:26-27, *"Now in the sixth month, the angel Gabriel was sent from God to a city of Galilee named Nazareth, ²⁷ to a virgin pledged to be married to a man whose name was Joseph, of David's house. The virgin's name was Mary."*

Yet again, in verses twenty-six and twenty-seven, the word virgin in Greek is the word **Parthenos,** which can refer to a young maiden, virgin, or unmarried woman as we just reviewed in Matthew, keep this in mind.

Luke Chapter 1:28, *"Having come in, the angel said to her, "Rejoice, you highly favored one! The Lord is with you. Blessed are you among women!"*

The word favored in this twenty-eighth verse is the transliterated Greek word ***charitoo,*** which means to make graceful, to endow with grace and more specifically, to make accepted. This word is used only one other time in the Bible and that is in Ephesians chapter one when Paul is speaking regarding our redemption through Jesus.

Ephesians 1:6,

"to the praise of the glory of his grace, by which he freely gave us favor in the Beloved."

I will remind us all of the point of this chapter. In the beginning, I started by giving examples of grace provided to a few persons in the Bible (Paul and Jonah). Please pay attention to this section as I will explain how God gave Mary grace and she bore Jesus.

Luke Chapter 1:29, ***"But when she saw him, she was greatly troubled at the saying, and considered what kind of salutation this might be."***

The first thing the angel Gabriel does when he sees Mary in verse twenty-eight is give her a pleasant greeting and tell her she is highly favored. However, in verse twenty-nine, we are told Mary was troubled by the words the angel said to her. Although she may be nervous regarding his presence, this is not stated to us. The focus is on Mary being troubled specifically by the angels' words.
I believe that the discomfort Mary is experiencing due to the angel's kind words to her are attributed to feelings of unworthiness caused by Mary being with child and betrothed. This can be deemed as speculation, which I don't deny; however, we will go over some information that has led me to this conclusion in a bit.

Luke Chapter 1:30, ***"The angel said to her, "Don't be afraid, Mary, for you have found favor with God."***

In Luke 1 verse thirty, the angel Gabriel tells Mary she has found favor with God. The transliterated Greek word for favor in this verse is *charis.* One of this word's primary purposes for use is to show God's mercy on us. In my opinion, God is showing Mary mercy.

This is another point that we will go deeper into when we are further down in this chapter, particularly starting with verse forty-eight when we get to Mary's song of Praise to the Lord. For now, we will continue with the breakdown of Lukes chapter 1 in its consecutive order as there are points to be made in these verses as well.

Luke chapter 1 verse thirty-one,

"Behold, you will conceive in your womb and give birth to a son, and shall name him 'Jesus.'"

The transliterated Greek word used in verse thirty-one for conceive is **sullambano,** which means to collect, to take, by implication, to take part with, to assist, or to conceive. This word is used about sixteen times in the New Testament, and in several of these verses, it is described as an act of seizing, taking, or helping.

The word **sullambano** in this verse reveals that Mary will *help* in bringing forth Jesus, not create him. She will give birth to the vessel He will use. How can we come to this conclusion? We can say this due to Jesus already existing, which we went over in the Old Testament. This conclusion can also be drawn due to the following verse.

Hebrews 7:3,

"without father, without mother, without genealogy, having neither beginning of days nor end of life, but made like the Son of God), remains a priest continually."

This verse states the likeness of Melchizedek to Jesus. Melchizedek was the King of Salem whom Abraham briefly encountered in the book of Genesis; no lineage record is recorded. The comparison is that Jesus has no father or mother just as Melchizedek did not have as well.

Luke 1 verse 32-33,

"He will be great and will be called the Son of the Most High. The Lord God will give him the throne of his father David, ³³ and he will reign over the house of Jacob forever. There will be no end to his Kingdom."

The angel Gabriel informs Mary that she will bring forth a son, and He will be holy. He will be called the Son of the Most High and reign over Jacob's house forever.

Luke 1:34,

Translation Greek to English: *"Said then Mary to the angel, how will be this, since a man not I know?"*

The word "know" in verse thirty-four is the same Greek word as in Matthew 1:25: **ginosko,** meaning to come to know, recognize, or perceive. As previously said, this transliterated Greek word **ginosko** is used over two hundred times in the New Testament. It does not give any sexual context except for Matthew 1:25 and Luke 1:34. As I recognized prior, I do not deny that this word can be used to refer to sexual relations; however, using the word **ginosko** as a sexual reference in these two Scriptures is not proper in my view. This word can be used to express a knowing of someone in an experiential way not conclusively meaning sexually.

Staying in context, Mary and Joseph have not had their wedding ceremony, which is one of the final steps to completing the marriage. Therefore, leaving room to interpret the word **ginosko** used in this part of scripture to mean the betrothed couple has not come to fully acknowledge each other as husband and wife. It is plausible to interpret this Greek word in those two passages as regarding Mary and Joseph not yet assembling via their wedding ceremony and living together instead of in a sexual context.

Luke 1:35, *"The angel answered her, "The Holy Spirit will come on you, and the power of the Most High will overshadow you.*

Therefore also the holy one who is born from you will be called the Son of God."

The angel Gabriel explains how the vessel will be holy and called the Son of God by saying the Holy Spirit will come upon her and the power of the Most High will overshadow her.

The angel is not explaining how the vessel will be created. This is what causes Mary confusion. She is puzzled about how the child would be holy, great, and called the Son of the Most High when she is "betrothed" and with child.

In verse 36, the angel Gabriel explains to Mary that her cousin Elizabeth is with child (six months pregnant) in her old age, and she is called barren. In verse thirty-seven, the angel Gabriel states that nothing is impossible with God.

Then, in verse thirty-eight, Mary rejoices, stating, "Be it unto me according to thy word, and the angel departed from her."

In verses 39-43 Mary goes to see her cousin Elizabeth after having been visited by the angel Gabriel. The Holy Spirit fills Elizabeth, pregnant with John the Baptist, and she proclaims the below Bible verse.

Luke 1:43, "**Why am I so favored, that the mother of my Lord should come to me?**"

I will acknowledge this verse soon.

Now, we will break down Mary's Song of Praise and why it provides more depth into Mary's grace.

Luke 1:46-55

"And Mary said:
"My soul magnifies the Lord.
47   My spirit has rejoiced in God my Savior,
48   for he has looked at the humble state of his servant.
For behold, from now on, all generations will call me blessed.

⁴⁹   For he who is mighty has done great things for me.
   Holy is his name.
⁵⁰   His mercy is for generations and generations on those who fear him.
⁵¹ He has shown strength with his arm.
   He has scattered the proud in the imagination of their hearts.
⁵² He has put down princes from their thrones,
   and has exalted the lowly.
⁵³ He has filled the hungry with good things.
   He has sent the rich away empty.
⁵⁴ He has given help to Israel, his servant, that he might remember mercy,
⁵⁵   as he spoke to our fathers,
   to Abraham and his offspring forever.".

In this section of scripture, I find Mary to be a great comparison to Hannah in 1 Samuel chapter 1:12; nothing has changed in her immediate view; however, after she prayed and Eli told her, "Go in peace: and the God of Israel grant thee thy petition that thou hast asked of him." She was overcome with the peace only God can give us. Look at verse forty-eight from Mary's Song of Praise.

Parallel Translation Greek to English: Luke 1:48 **"For He has looked upon the humiliation of the handmaiden of Him. Behold for from henceforth will count blessed me all the generations."**

Now Mary is referring to herself and stating that God has saw her humiliation. When we reach the last portion of this verse saying, *"Behold for from henceforth will count blessed me all the generations."* We can view this statement from Mary within the context that we have been following, which would conclude that her gratefulness would stem from God providing grace and mercy on her.
The word for humiliation in Luke 1:48 is the transliterated Greek word **tapeinósis** and is defined as a state of being brought down low. It comes

from the word ***tapeinoó*** meaning to depress or humiliate particularly in the form of ranking; while the word ***tapeinósis*** can be used in a metaphorical manner, it is being utilized in a literal sense in this verse.

This gives us the okay to stay within our context of Mary feeling unworthiness when the angel Gabriel greets her and says she has found grace with God. Why, because in her song of praise she admits to being in this state in verse forty-eight, bringing it to a full circle with the reasoning of the word ***charitoó*** used in Luke 1:28. This word choice shows that the angel is addressing that Mary is accepted. However, after the angel tells her this, Mary is troubled by this in verse twenty-nine. So, in verse thirty, the word ***charis*** being used by the angel is conveying that God has had mercy on her.

Remember, in her song of praise, she says God's mercy is on those who fear Him. Though this can be viewed as general we cannot discount the fact that this is her song of praise to God, expressing what He has done for her. You may not view this as such, but again, if we are continuing to put the whole chapter into context, the meaning behind the angel's words when telling her she has found favor with God or "***charis***" which is often used to show God's mercy; follows this concept with her song of praise as well as the other information we have just reviewed.

So, let's put all this together. The angel Gabriel visits Mary; he greets her and tells her she is highly favored. The word choice in verse twenty-eight for favor means to be made accepted. In verse twenty-nine Mary is troubled by the angel's words and in verse thirty the angel explains to her that God has had mercy on her as that is one of the main uses regarding the word choice for favor in that verse and makes sense to use as such for this context. In verse 48 of Mary's song of praise, she states that God has seen her humiliation. The word choice for humiliation in Greek leads us to believe that this is a literal state that Mary was in and not just putting herself into a humble position. Paying attention to the specific words chosen for each of these verses in the Greek language, it is safe to stay within our context that Mary was concerned about suffering continued humiliation because she has thanked God for seeing it and now, she is blessed.

Mary was in a state of humiliation due to her being pregnant and betrothed. She risked further humiliation from her family, Joseph's family, and their community. This is consistent with what Joseph's concerns were regarding Mary being at risk for disgrace. Notably, understanding the information in this context also clarifies that Mary (just like Joseph) is shown to be concerned with humiliation and not her life being in jeopardy. Why? There is no law that details consequences for a betrothed couple having relations before the wedding ceremony. Again, of course this was not an accepted practice, but it did not have a legal death penalty attached to it as committing adultery did. Mary and Joseph know that she had not committed adultery so they were not concerned with the consequences surrounding that, but rather shame for coming together with one another before they should have.

We must ask ourselves, if Mary were not pregnant before the angel came to her, why would she be in this state of humiliation already? Mary most likely told Joseph she was pregnant before the angel came to visit either of them, seeing as though Joseph was devising a plan so she would not be humiliated. For Joseph to take Mary as his wife, they were required to attend public events which would have exposed the fact that she was pregnant before the official marriage.

On many occasions, the Bible uses the meek to magnify God's name and glory. One of the biggest purposes of God doing this is to provide clarity that He cares for all and looks first in the heart of man. This situation is no different. Jesus stating in Matthew 9:13 that He desires mercy, not sacrifice and He was not called to the righteous but has come for sinners, connects this interpretation even deeper. He was sent through Mary because she had flaws but our society believes the opposite, that Mary was so pure and that God rewarded her with carrying Jesus. This brings us back to the Greek word ***charitoó*** only being used in Luke 1:28 and Ephesians 1:6 to highlight our redemption through Jesus being given to us freely and not because we have earned it.

How is this Considered a Parable?

A parable is a story with an important message and a lesson that should change how we view and or act in certain situations. It reveals God's character and shows how we are to carry ourselves.

Why can Mary and Joseph's story qualify as a parable? Primarily, the interpretation presented in this book is not seen at first glance; it must be reviewed and confirmed by God, as the disciples sometimes had to ask Jesus to reveal the true meaning of some of his teachings privately. This parable will not make sense to many simply because their religious views will interfere with the true meaning of it. It takes a humble and pure heart to set aside judgment and religious righteousness to discern it.

Many of us still view the narrow path incorrectly; we see it as full of fasting, following commandments, and continuing religious rituals. This path has room for our flaws if we seek God to make real changes in the behaviors and mindsets that make us disobedient to His Word. True repentance asks and allows God to guide our steps because we have realized we do not have all the answers.

It may sometimes feel like a burden or a to-do list; however, when we truly submit to God it is something we want and continuously choose to do because we love Him. We recognize that God leading our path will bring prosperity far beyond what we can imagine. Prosperity comes in many forms. Peace of mind can allow one to flourish through life's trials more than receiving tangible items such as currency. When deprived, knowing you are protected and safe is a prosperous and joyous feeling. Prosperity is having true intimacy with God while continuously nurturing that relationship. When we know this, our burdens are lighter, leaving room for the joy of the Lord and fulfillment in what He has called us to steward for His name's sake.

The fruit of God's word to Mary and Joseph that is recognizable to them both, is that they were not overtaken by shame or humiliation from their people. If we study the Scripture and hone in on what exactly the two of them were afraid of, it was fear of Mary being disgraced publicly, and this fear did not come to pass; we see the opposite with others that Mary encounters, giving her acclamations regarding her situation and affirming God's word that Jesus was of importance. The fruit of God's word to the people was the coming of Jesus fulfilling the prophecy in Isaiah 7:14 stating that the young woman will conceive and bear a son and His name shall be Immanuel which means, "God is with us."

Many of us find this ultimate parable difficult to decipher because we often place our views on how we believe God will go about His own will. For something to be credible enough to elicit our respect, it must check every box in a list of righteous requirements in the way we define them. God is not obligated to cultivate His will in a way that we can always comprehend. At times, it will surpass our understanding and that is okay. We should get comfortable with the truth that we will never know everything; however, it is vitally important that we seek God to learn and understand the things He wants to reveal to us, then place our focus on advancing the kingdom. We as humans often try to dictate what is worthy of grace and what qualifies as a miracle. Our ability to breathe is a miracle. The human body is so intricate that no person could have considered all the necessary things for our bodies to work together daily and achieve something as simple as breathing correctly. There is not one person on earth that can explain from start to finish every area of the body, how it was created and how it functions. We have so many specialties and sub-specialties in the medical world because our human minds cannot withstand what it would take to retain all the knowledge and skills needed to fully understand the human body God created for us. Do not let anyone deceive you into thinking any human on earth could ever comprehend every aspect of God. We cannot even comprehend every aspect of ourselves.

God coming to earth to save us from our sins when He did not have to is the miracle, not the virgin birth. This was the ultimate act of love. Many of us are more intrigued with the supposed supernatural implications of this beautiful account. We are not as grateful as we should be for God's sacrifice, leading us to give glory to humans over God. God shares His glory with no one.

Mary is not to be worshiped; she is an example of God's grace. It is a beautiful entrance into the New Testament and the foreshadowing that sets the tone for what Jesus was sent to earth to accomplish, presenting God's gift of grace/mercy to us when we did not deserve it. The importance of Mary and Joseph's story is the Grace of God not miracles and wonders.

Here Jesus redirects a woman to what is most important and what we should be focused on.

Luke 11:27-28,

"It came to pass, as he said these things, a certain woman out of the multitude lifted up her voice and said to him, "Blessed is the womb that bore you, and the breasts which nursed you!"

²⁸ But he said, "On the contrary, blessed are those who hear the word of God, and keep it!"

As you are taking in all this information, I would like you to also keep in mind that while there is a well-known argument for the virgin birth theory, there is also a powerful case for these details presented to you today. Nowhere in the Bible does it confirm that Mary gave birth to Jesus due to a virgin birth outside of the Scriptures we have dissected in the book of Isaiah and the gospels of Matthew and Luke. This gives credibility to the information I have laid out here. Whether you conclude this reasoning is sufficient or faulty, I pray you continue researching this topic after reading this book and remember this verse.

Hebrews 7:3

"without father, without mother, without genealogy, having neither beginning of days nor end of life, but made like the Son of God), remains a priest continually."

Jesus is without a father or mother. How could this Bible verse be plausible if the information I provided here were not true?
If we say Jesus is without a father or mother because God impregnated Mary, it is inaccurate. This only explains how Jesus does not have an earthly father and implies that He has an earthly mother, therefore invalidating the Scripture. In the next chapter of this book, I will explain how we can agree with this verse without any lingering thoughts of doubt.
This concept may be difficult to grasp. We all will wrestle with

certain things regarding the bible. If you have never experienced this, you are not reading your Bible enough. Many of us will experience a lack of faith or some sense of unbelief. This leads me to the next point of why the *Ultimate Parable* is so difficult to decipher.

Let us review the following passage,

Luke 2:48–50. Jesus stayed behind in Jerusalem after the day feast of the Passover, which His parents Mary, and Joseph, were unaware of. After three days of searching, His parents found Him in a temple listening to/asking questions to the teachers.

"When they saw him, they were astonished; and his mother said to him, "Son, why have you treated us this way? Behold, your father and I were anxiously looking for you."

[49] *He said to them, "Why were you looking for me? Didn't you know that I must be in my Father's house?"* [50] *They didn't understand the saying which he spoke to them."*

Mary and Joseph are in a state of confusion and this is also something we see with Jesus's disciples. Jesus performed so many miracles before their eyes, yet in times of uncertainty, the disciples had no faith. Moments such as Jesus calming a storm while He and the disciples were on the boat.

Mark 4:35-41

"On that day, when evening had come, he said to them, "Let's go over to the other side." [36] *Leaving the multitude, they took him with them, even as he was, in the boat. Other small boats were also with him.* [37] *A big wind storm arose, and the waves beat into the boat, so much that the boat was already filled.* [38] *He himself was in the stern, asleep on the cushion; and they woke him up and asked him, "Teacher, don't you care that we are dying?"*

³⁹ He awoke and rebuked the wind, and said to the sea, "Peace! Be still!" The wind ceased and there was a great calm. ⁴⁰ He said to them, "Why are you so afraid? How is it that you have no faith?"

⁴¹ They were greatly afraid and said to one another, "Who then is this, that even the wind and the sea obey him!"

Just like the disciples, Mary had the truth right before her. She was told that the vessel would be called the Son of the Most High, however, she did not have a full understanding of it. So many had spoken in high regard about Jesus, the angel announcing Jesus's birth and calling him Christ the Lord in Luke 2:11, and the shepherds delivering this message to Mary. Simeon in Luke, chapter 2:27–35 as well. Also, returning to Luke 1:43 when Elizabeth was filled with the Holy Spirit and called Mary the mother of her Lord. Sometimes, even when the truth is right in front of us if we cannot comprehend it, we create an alternative meaning easier to digest.

In the scripture we just read (Luke 2:48-50), Mary and Joseph are confused that Jesus is saying they should have known He would be in His Father's house. It is subtle, but I pray you caught it.

Again, Mary did not understand the weight of what was told to her regarding Jesus being the Son of God. A lot of us can relate to this. God will tell us something, and we view it with our human minds and not our spiritual sight, and in the end, we are surprised and amazed by the outcome that God gives us, one that we could have never imagined. God gives us the ending and provides us with pieces along the way. We start collecting pieces that we think are not relevant to the picture God showed us; however, little do we know, the picture is much larger and magnificent than we could ever imagine. We are in awe when He is finished guiding our path to the promises He has given us.

Let us be honest; if Mary fully understood that she was carrying God in her womb at the time of her pregnancy, she would have been anxious every day. She knew that the child she had was divine but not God in the flesh. Others have been referred to as sons of God, particularly in Hosea 1:10-11. God says the nation of Israel will be called "the sons of the living

God;" so Mary hearing the angel Gabriel say it, likely did not register to her in the way the angel truly meant. We will dive deeper into the meaning of the Son as it pertains to Jesus in a little while.

God knows how much we can manage. He tells the truth in a way that we will not be overburdened with the information as we are consistently taking actions to the steps He lays out for us. God will not put more on us than we can bear because we can always bear it when we cast it unto Him and follow His lead.

It is amazing how God will tell us a thing, and most times, we do not perceive it correctly until it is in front of us; sadly, some do not experience the revelation at all.

It is so difficult for many of us to realize that even though we may fall short in our walk sometimes, God judges us by our hearts and forgives us, making us new creatures striving to walk with Him and adjust our actions to His will. We cannot accept this interpretation because we do not feel worthy of this magnitude of love God can provide us with.

Chapter Three

Clarity and the Importance of Jesus's Way into the World

There is not one instance where someone in the Bible refers to Mary as the woman who had a virgin birth after Jesus was born. Wouldn't an event like that have some form of notoriety, even if it were just in her local area? We would think that this event would confirm Jesus's Deity. Jesus would have been deemed divine simply due to this event alone, right? It may be true for many; however, even some who believe in the virgin birth still do not see Jesus as who He truly is. This brings us back to Mark 6:1-6

"He went out from there. He came into his own country, and his disciples followed him. ² When the Sabbath had come, he began to teach in the synagogue, and many hearing him were astonished, saying, "Where did this man get these things?" and, "What is the wisdom that is given to this man, that such mighty works come about by his hands? ³ Isn't this the carpenter, the son of Mary and brother of James, Joses, Judah, and Simon? Aren't his sisters here with us?" So they were offended at him.

⁴ Jesus said to them, "A prophet is not without honor, except in his own country, and among his own relatives, and in his own house." ⁵ He could do no mighty work there, except that he laid his hands on a few sick people and healed them. ⁶ He marveled because of their unbelief."

His people did not believe partially because there was no virgin birth. Jesus was born in an earthly way. He came here in a very humble state as He lived His life. His entrance into the world via a virgin birth does not correlate with the character Jesus displayed on Earth. When we read Scripture during Jesus's ministry, He tells quite a few people not to reveal who He is once they experience revelation regarding His Deity. Only those with eyes to see and ears to hear will realize who He is. One example is found in Mark chapter 9:1-9 when Jesus Transfigures on the Mount.

While reading this book, unfortunately, many will let their flesh and mind dictate the meaning behind these words. They will walk in their earthly wisdom instead of allowing the Holy Spirit to minister to them as they read and do their research along the way.

Jesus came to earth to save us from death and sin, as we discussed earlier.

Hebrews 2:14-18

"Since then the children have shared in flesh and blood, he also himself in the same way partook of the same, that through death he

might bring to nothing him who had the power of death, that is, the devil, ⁱ⁵ and might deliver all of them who through fear of death were all their lifetime subject to bondage. ¹⁶ For most certainly, he doesn't give help to angels, but he gives help to the offspring of Abraham. ¹⁷ Therefore he was obligated in all things to be made like his brothers, that he might become a merciful and faithful high priest in things pertaining to God, to make atonement for the sins of the people. ¹⁸ For in that he himself has suffered being tempted, he is able to help those who are tempted."

When studying the hypostatic union of Jesus, it is important that we end our studies with clarity.
Jesus was one hundred percent human and one hundred percent God. Let us ask ourselves, how would Jesus have been considered one hundred percent human if the vessel He used on earth was divinely created by God and placed in Mary's womb?

Jesus came from the seed of David.

In 2 Samuel chapter 7, David wants to build a house for God. God tells the prophet Nathan to inform David he does not need to make Him a house. However, God is pleased that Daivd has thought of Him this way and tells Nathen to speak these words to David. Verse 12-17

"When your days are fulfilled and you sleep with your fathers, I will set up your offspring after you, who will proceed out of your body, and I will establish his kingdom. ¹³ He will build a house for my name, and I will establish the throne of his kingdom forever. ¹⁴ I will be his father, and he will be my son. If he commits iniquity, I will chasten him with the rod of men and with the stripes of the children of men; ¹⁵ but my loving kindness will not depart from him, as I took it from Saul, whom I put away before you. ¹⁶ Your house and your kingdom will be made sure forever before you. Your throne will be established forever.""" ¹⁷ Nathan spoke to David all

these words, and according to all this vision."

In the above Scripture, God is speaking of Soloman and Jesus; Soloman will be the one to build God's physical house; Jesus will be the one to build the spiritual house that is the church. Jesus is of David's seed as well as Soloman. This fact is mentioned several times; for example, the above verse we just reviewed in 2 Samuel 7:12–17 and the below verse. Romans 1:3-4,

"concerning his Son, who was born of the offspring of David according to the flesh, ⁴ who was declared to be the Son of God with power according to the Spirit of holiness, by the resurrection from the dead, Jesus Christ our Lord,"

Jesus came to earth and followed earthly ways until his reveal (ministry) after fasting and being baptized. This is why we can place all our trust in Him. He sacrificed His divinity in every way to save us. He knows firsthand what temptation feels like and understands the emotions we go through and why He is our Priest.

Again, while following this book, review the Scriptures for yourself, as I will not go through all passages about each topic discussed. Seeking God's clarity for yourself is important, as you will have peace in your spirit if your clarity is confirmed directly from Him.

Why is it so important that we know that Jesus was not born of a virgin? As some may attribute Jesus' Deity to His virgin birth, I believe that the virgin birth theory weakens the validity of Jesus's true nature. Jesus was here before all creation, and He is God in the flesh.

Example: John 8:48-59

"Then the Jews answered him, "Don't we say well that you are a Samaritan, and have a demon?"

⁴⁹ Jesus answered, "I don't have a demon, but I honor my Father and you dishonor me. ⁵⁰ But I don't seek my own glory. There is one who seeks and judges. ⁵¹ Most certainly, I tell you, if a person keeps my word, he will never see death."

⁵² Then the Jews said to him, "Now we know that you have a demon. Abraham died, as did the prophets; and you say, 'If a man keeps my word, he will never taste of death.' ⁵³ Are you greater than our father Abraham, who died? The prophets died. Who do you make yourself out to be?"

⁵⁴ Jesus answered, "If I glorify myself, my glory is nothing. It is my Father who glorifies me, of whom you say that he is our God. ⁵⁵ You have not known him, but I know him. If I said, 'I don't know him,' I would be like you, a liar. But I know him and keep his word. ⁵⁶ Your father Abraham rejoiced to see my day. He saw it and was glad."

⁵⁷ The Jews therefore said to him, "You are not yet fifty years old! Have you seen Abraham?"

⁵⁸ Jesus said to them, "Most certainly, I tell you, before Abraham came into existence, I AM."

⁵⁹ Therefore they took up stones to throw at him, but Jesus hid himself and went out of the temple, having gone through the middle of them, and so passed by."

    The Jewish people knew that Jesus was proclaiming to be God; this is why they were so angry and why they would eventually advocate for His crucifixion under Roman authority.
By trying to justify the virgin birth theory, you are indirectly bringing a false form of validation to anyone saying Jesus did not exist before Mary bore Him and that He is not God in the flesh.
We are attributing the creation of Jesus to the Father, which implies Jesus is not God. How? By stating that God placed Jesus in Mary's womb without any male reproduction assistance and attesting that this is how

God is Jesus's Father is an extremely poor interpretation that leads to so many seeds of doubt about Jesus's Deity. By stating this, you are implying there was no seed of David used, which is inaccurate because, again, Jesus had to be one hundred percent human to save all of us.

Romans 8:3-4,

"For what the law couldn't do, in that it was weak through the flesh, God did, sending his own Son in the likeness of sinful flesh and for sin, he condemned sin in the flesh, ⁴ that the ordinance of the law might be fulfilled in us who don't walk according to the flesh, but according to the Spirit."

Jesus used a vessel from the seed of David through Joseph and came into the earth from the womb of Mary.
Why would the entire Bible take this amount of effort in stating Jesus's lineage and tracking the line in so much detail for Jesus's vessel not to be a part of the bloodline of David as God said it would?

I would like to add that I am not here to argue regarding Matthew and Luke's genealogy accounts regarding Joseph's lineage to David, as there have been prior disputes concerning these two gospels' dissection of the actual father of Joseph. You can find a couple of viewpoints in the book The Case for Christ (Strobel, 1998). The simple fact that Joseph is of the line of David needs to be considered now.

Some believe that Mary is from David's bloodline as well. Historically, generations were traced through the male's genealogy to depict lineage, so the accounts for the bloodline are written from the perspective of Joseph and not Mary. Honestly, there is no way of knowing that Mary is of the line of David with one hundred percent certainty; however, the Bible clearly states that Joseph is of the line of David several times, and it does not repeatedly state this fact just for fun.

Matthew 1:16-17

"Jacob became the father of Joseph, the husband of Mary, from whom was born Jesus, who is called Christ.

17 So all the generations from Abraham to David are fourteen generations; from David to the exile to Babylon fourteen generations; and from the carrying away to Babylon to the Christ, fourteen generations."

Luke 1:27

"Now in the sixth month, the angel Gabriel was sent from God to a city of Galilee named Nazareth, 27 to a virgin pledged to be married to a man whose name was Joseph, of David's house. The virgin's name was Mary."

Luke 2:4-5

Joseph also went up from Galilee, out of the city of Nazareth, into Judea, to David's city, which is called Bethlehem, because he was of the house and family of David, 5 to enroll himself with Mary, who was pledged to be married to him as wife, being pregnant."

<u>Jesus, God in the flesh</u>

We touched on this topic in the Prelude of *Getting to Know Jesus;* we will continue here with a few scriptures. I would like you to read them, meditate on them, and seek the Lord so that you may conclude whether you believe that Jesus is God in the flesh.

Philippians 2:1-11

"If therefore there is any exhortation in Christ, if any consolation of love, if any fellowship of the Spirit, if any tender mercies and compassion, 2 make my joy full by being like-minded, having the same love, being of one accord, of one mind; 3 doing nothing through rivalry or through conceit, but in humility, each counting others better than himself; 4 each of you not just looking to his own things, but each of you also to the things of others.

⁵ Have this in your mind, which was also in Christ Jesus, ⁶ who, existing in the form of God, didn't consider equality with God a thing to be grasped, ⁷ but emptied himself, taking the form of a servant, being made in the likeness of men. ⁸ And being found in human form, he humbled himself, becoming obedient to the point of death, yes, the death of the cross. ⁹ Therefore God also highly exalted him, and gave to him the name which is above every name, ¹⁰ that at the name of Jesus every knee should bow, of those in heaven, those on earth, and those under the earth, ¹¹ and that every tongue should confess that Jesus Christ is Lord, to the glory of God the Father."

Acts 20:28,

Take heed, therefore, to yourselves and to all the flock, in which the Holy Spirit has made you overseers, to shepherd the assembly of the Lord and God which he purchased with his own blood.

It says God purchased the assembly aka the church with His own blood. Jesus used His blood to save us; this means that Jesus is God in the flesh.

Son of the Most High

I previously mentioned that Mary did not fully understand what the angel Gabriel meant when calling Jesus, the Son of the Most High. Provided here is a way to understand that Jesus is not being referred to as the physical Son of God but the true nature of God.

Two of the most used words for son in the New Testament are the Greek words **huios** and **teknon**; while both can refer to a child or son, the word **huios** is the only word ever used to describe Jesus except in Luke 2:48, when Mary and Joseph find Jesus in the Temple, the Greek word for son here is **teknon**. We discussed this verse previously when acknowledging Mary's lack of understanding of who Jesus is, and I will bring my point home here.

Luke 2:48-49

"When they saw him, they were astonished; and his mother said to him, "Son, why have you treated us this way? Behold, your father and I were anxiously looking for you."

[49] He said to them, "Why were you looking for me? Didn't you know that I must be in my Father's house?"

The word **teknon** typically describes a child sharing the bloodline of a parent. The word **huios** is mainly used when trying to convey that a person has the character of a parent, not necessarily from blood but in a spiritual sense of having the same nature, it can be indiscernible as far as the qualities between the two. This is the word always used about Jesus. Whether Jesus was being called the Son of Man, Son of God, or it is referring to him as an infant, or adult, the translation for Son is always the Greek word **huios**. Except in the verse, we just read. Mary is describing Jesus as her **teknon** in this scripture. She has the understanding that Jesus is her and Joseph's biological son, but again, she does not fully understand what God was doing when He saved her from humiliation.

This exemplifies how we can be so close to God and still fall short if we rely on our own understanding. When Mary and Joseph found their Son in the Temple, and Jesus stated that they should have known He would be in His Father's House, Jesus was attempting to reveal His true relationship with The Father. However, Mary and Joseph are not catching it. They are still viewing Jesus as just their son and not God. Hence, Jesus saying He was in His father's house, and it is not connecting to Joseph in anyway puzzled them both.

This is the same experience many of the people of that time had. They were not looking for God in the flesh even though the angel said all this took place and they shall call Him Immanuel which means "God is with us." Many did not conclude that God would be with them in a literal sense. The majority of them were looking for an actual King in their time to rule over them and when they did not acquire the King in the way they wanted, they were not open to receiving Jesus for who He actually was.

Again, when defining revelation, we can state that it must be something that was always true, however, the one receiving it is now able to view it correctly. It does not always mean you have never heard these words before; it means this is your first time being able to properly comprehend what is being revealed. But as Luke 2:50 states, Joseph and Mary did not grasp the true meaning of His words neither did most of the people of that time.

Luke 2:50

"They didn't understand the saying which he spoke to them."

We reviewed my thoughts on the different versions of the Bible at the beginning of this book. How the Holy Spirit revealed the meaning behind this portion of Scripture to me (Luke 2:48-50) is a good example of my perspective on God allowing things to be situated so that we can only come to Him for confirmation and clarification. Everything serves a purpose in His plan. The breakdown of this one Scripture alone tied so much together.

I would like to bring attention to the fact that children of God are described as **huios** a few times in the Bible; this shows the character we are to uphold by reflecting God's traits on earth. However, **teknon,** which mainly refers to the biological status of a child or offspring, is also used for us. This leads some to think that the words are interchangeable, and they are to an extent. The point of providing the knowledge that Jesus is never referred to as **teknon** in the Bible but only **huios** again, adds validity to Jesus's statement of being one with the Father in John 10:29-30.

Any verse in the Bible that shows Jesus appearing to be unequal to the Father while on earth is correct. Jesus lowered Himself to save us.

Hebrews 2:9-10

"But we see him who has been made a little lower than the angels, Jesus, because of the suffering of death crowned with glory and honor, that by the grace of God he should taste of death for everyone.

¹⁰ For it became him, for whom are all things and through whom are all things, in bringing many children to glory, to make the author of their salvation perfect through sufferings."

Philippians 2:5-8

"Have this in your mind, which was also in Christ Jesus, ⁶ who, existing in the form of God, didn't consider equality with God a thing to be grasped, ⁷ but emptied himself, taking the form of a servant, being made in the likeness of men. ⁸ And being found in human form, he humbled himself, becoming obedient to the point of death, yes, the death of the cross."

However, the Old Testament never sees Jesus as unequal to the Father. When Jesus appears in the Old Testament, He is called God (YHWH) several times.

You can review the previous Bible Scriptures provided at the beginning of the book in Chapter 1 shedding light on Jesus's appearance in the Old Testament. Again, I advise you to ask the Holy Spirit to guide your studies and remove any known or unknown bias in your heart. For now, look at one more example from Scripture.

Genesis 22:11-18

"Yahweh's angel called to him out of the sky, and said, "Abraham, Abraham!"

He said, "Here I am."

12 He said, "Don't lay your hand on the boy or do anything to him. For now I know that you fear God, since you have not withheld your son, your only son, from me."

13 Abraham lifted up his eyes, and looked, and saw that behind him was a ram caught in the thicket by his horns. Abraham went and took the ram, and offered him up for a burnt offering instead of his son. 14 Abraham called the name of that place "Yahweh Will Provide". As it is said to this day, "On Yahweh's mountain, it will be provided."

15 Yahweh's angel called to Abraham a second time out of the sky, 16 and said, "'I have sworn by myself,' says Yahweh, 'because you have done this thing, and have not withheld your son, your only son, 17 that I will bless you greatly, and I will multiply your offspring greatly like the stars of the heavens, and like the sand which is on the seashore. Your offspring will possess the gate of his enemies. 18 All the nations of the earth will be blessed by your offspring, because you have obeyed my voice.'"

In this portion of Scripture, God reveals to Abraham that he will not be sacrificing his son; it was a test of faith. Note, that verse eleven is The Angel of the Lord speaking, which is Jesus. Verse 12 states

12 He said, "Don't lay your hand on the boy or do anything to him. For now I know that you fear God, since you have not withheld your son, your only son, from me."

The Angel of the Lord (Jesus) says, *"Since you have not withheld your son, your only son, from Me."* He does not say you have not withheld your only son, from *Him* or *God*. I pray you catch that; if not, I will expound more.

At the beginning of Genesis chapter 22:1-2, God told Abraham to sacrifice his son, not an angel or anyone else.

"After these things, God tested Abraham, and said to him, "Abraham!"

He said, "Here I am."

² He said, "Now take your son, your only son, Isaac, whom you love, and go into the land of Moriah. Offer him there as a burnt offering on one of the mountains which I will tell you of."

The Angel of the Lord's wording in Genesis 22:12 (which I will place again below) is critical to comprehend if you truly desire to properly connect dots to Jesus and His true Deity.

"He said, "Don't lay your hand on the boy or do anything to him. For now I know that you fear God, since you have not withheld your son, your only son, from me."

Once again, I recommend the book *The Deity of Jesus Christ in the Old and New Testaments* (Gurbikian, 2011).
If you are still skeptical about Jesus's true nature, here are some Bible verses that may help. Humans are to only worship God. People have been corrected for bowing down to angelic beings and other humans. Let us look at some examples.

Acts 10:24-27

"On the next day they entered into Caesarea. Cornelius was waiting for them, having called together his relatives and his near friends. ²⁵ When Peter entered, Cornelius met him, fell down at his feet, and worshiped him. ²⁶ But Peter raised him up, saying, "Stand up! I myself am also a man." ²⁷ As he talked with him, he went in and found many gathered together."

Revelation 22:6-9

"He said to me, "These words are faithful and true. The Lord God of the spirits of the prophets sent his angel to show to his bondservants the things which must happen soon."

⁷ "Behold, I am coming soon! Blessed is he who keeps the words of the prophecy of this book."

⁸ Now I, John, am the one who heard and saw these things. When I heard and saw, I fell down to worship before the feet of the angel who had shown me these things. ⁹ He said to me, "You must not do that! I am a fellow bondservant with you and with your brothers, the prophets, and with those who keep the words of this book. Worship God."

Jesus never rebuked anyone that worshiped Him, and God is the only one we are permitted to worship. Review Matthew Chapter 8:1-3, Mark Chapter 5:6-7 and John 9:35-38. There are several more examples showing Jesus is God, but I will end it with this Bible Scripture.

John 17:4-5

"I glorified you on the earth. I have accomplished the work which you have given me to do. ⁵ Now, Father, glorify me with your own self with the glory which I had with you before the world existed."

Hopefully, these powerful verses are a step toward your path to unveiling Jesus's true nature and being one with the Father if you do not already believe this is so.
Now, let us continue and review some information that proves Jesus not being born of a virgin does not dishonor Him in any way.
Jesus, not being born from a virgin in no way discredits His sinless nature. It in fact provides more clarity as to how much Jesus endured and the magnitude of love He has for us. We have gone over some of this information earlier, but I will reiterate.

Jesus did not have to be born of a virgin to ensure that He would not inherit the sins of His parents per Ezekiel 18:20. God's purity was not in jeopardy due to Him not being born of a virgin. God would still be pure no matter what vessel He chooses to dwell in because the vessel is not God; it represents Him in those moments. We are bearers of the image of God; however, we do sinful things due to our impure hearts and fleshly bodies but in no way due to God.

Romans 8:9-11

"But you are not in the flesh but in the Spirit, if it is so that the Spirit of God dwells in you. But if any man doesn't have the Spirit of Christ, he is not his. [10] If Christ is in you, the body is dead because of sin, but the spirit is alive because of righteousness. [11] But if the Spirit of him who raised up Jesus from the dead dwells in you, he who raised up Christ Jesus from the dead will also give life to your mortal bodies through his Spirit who dwells in you."

The bible says in Matthew 4:1,

"Then Jesus was led up by the Spirit into the wilderness to be tempted by the devil."

    A lot of us believe that Jesus was born of a virgin so that He would be sinless. If Joseph and Mary had not created Jesus's vessel, He would not have possessed the ability to be tempted, or it would be some form of Him being slightly tempted due to Him having one earthly parent.
This is incredibly significant, Jesus taking on flesh and leading a human existence while keeping Himself from sin is another amazing reason that we can put our trust in Him.
He was not born without the ability to be tempted but resisted temptation when it was presented to Him.
Stating that Jesus is sinless because of a virgin birth implies that we never had to worry about Jesus being tempted because His fleshly body was made sinless, so in concurrence with that fact, Jesus would not be capable of sinning.
    Jesus not being born from a virgin does not take away the fact that

He never sinned. As stated earlier, Jesus's purpose in coming to earth by the same means as the rest of humanity shows the true unwavering love and grace, He provides us with and a true understanding of us. I pray I am conveying this message so that everyone can grasp the significance of God's entrance into the world and why it came about in this specific manner.

2 Corinthians 5:21

"For him who knew no sin he made to be sin on our behalf, so that in him we might become the righteousness of God."

Hebrews 4:14-16

"Having then a great high priest who has passed through the heavens, Jesus, the Son of God, let's hold tightly to our confession. ¹⁵ For we don't have a high priest who can't be touched with the feeling of our infirmities, but one who has been in all points tempted like we are, yet without sin. ¹⁶ Let's therefore draw near with boldness to the throne of grace, that we may receive mercy and may find grace for help in time of need."

1 Peter 2:21-22

"For you were called to this, because Christ also suffered for us, leaving you an example, that you should follow his steps, ²² who didn't sin, "neither was deceit found in his mouth."

Jesus's blood was considered pure because He never sinned. Just as the Israelites would find an animal without a spot or blemish, Jesus had no spot, blemish, or defect when it came to sin and why His blood was worthy of sacrifice.

Ephesians 1:7,

"In him we have our redemption through his blood, the forgiveness

of our trespasses, according to the riches of his grace."

The beautiful thing about what Jesus has accomplished in showing us how to live is that He provided a chance for us to reclaim the eternal life that we were always meant to have so that even after death, we may live.

CONCLUSION

Thank you for finishing this book. I pray you review it repeatedly. These words have no malicious intent, and I am saddened that this book will offend many. But the fact is, every truth that God gives us will not be pleasing to our ears and sometimes we must be willing to be uncomfortable to be led to the truth. Again, this book aims to proclaim and reveal the true nature of Jesus as God in the flesh to those souls who God has assigned to me for His glory.

This book's objective is also to break us free of our religious minds and come into the freedom of knowing God's grace is for all who recognize His voice no matter their background. As stated earlier, Mary's gift of grace was to set the tone for everything Jesus was sent to earth to accomplish justification through faith. I ask God to provide you with whatever confirmations you need to have the eyes to see the message being told through me. I also ask that you go to Abba yourself for confirmation. Another prominent reason I was led to create this book is the number of souls that are turned away from God due to the perplexity of the virgin birth. This information is a key to unlocking more understanding. God does not desire for us to be confused. I pray that this book brings more clarity to His purpose and allows many more of His children to place their complete trust in Him. Those who genuinely want to give God all of them but have sincere questions that need to be answered to build their faith. It is also for some people who are currently in an idolatrous relationship, whether within a religion, cult, or themselves. You are being called to reevaluate your current belief system, and with a pure and humble heart, be open to receiving correction and confirmation so God can guide you to the true path He has laid out for you.

    I have had my time to wrestle with this information and went through doubts, fear, and asking why God chose me to deliver this message in this way. The simple answer for that is because He said so, and whenever God leads us, it is always for the best. We must become comfortable doing God's work, anticipate suffering to glorify His name, and not always see the result because we trust what He is doing. Often, the calling God has for you will be completely out of your comfort zone but also something you receive true joy from. After I overcame the fear, the thought of introducing others to the love of Christ, the peace of God, and the mercy He provides filled me with an overwhelming amount of happiness. The message of Jesus being God has been proclaimed and shown through the Bible repeatedly and also by much literary works. However the gospel must continue being spread until all come into this knowing, and I am grateful to do my part. I pray you have experienced it through this book. Thank you!

I would like all of us to take a moment and thank our Father in Heaven for the grace He has provided us. Please read the Scripture below.

Galatians 5:19-21

"Now the deeds of the flesh are obvious, which are: adultery, sexual immorality, uncleanness, lustfulness, [20] idolatry, sorcery, hatred, strife, jealousies, outbursts of anger, rivalries, divisions, heresies, [21] envy, murders, drunkenness, orgies, and things like these; of which I forewarn you, even as I also forewarned you, that those who practice such things will not inherit God's Kingdom."

Romans 3:22-23

"even the righteousness of God through faith in Jesus Christ to all and on all those who believe. For there is no distinction, ²³ for all have sinned, and fall short of the glory of God;"

We all, at one point or another have committed one of these works of the flesh, and by God being just, we should not inherit the kingdom. But He knew that we could not save ourselves, so He became one of us to carry our burdens and showed us how we are to live. Now the only burden we bear is learning to trust Him completely, which is not a burden at all but a gift. We are always craving confirmation that the ones around us are trustworthy, and we have that in Him.

Matthew 11:28-30

"Come to me, all you who labor and are heavily burdened, and I will give you rest. ²⁹ Take my yoke upon you and learn from me, for I am gentle and humble in heart; and you will find rest for your souls. ³⁰ For my yoke is easy, and my burden is light."

Romans 5:8

"But God commends his own love toward us, in that while we were yet sinners, Christ died for us."

There is no work that we can do to save ourselves.

Romans 4:4-5

"Now to him who works, the reward is not counted as grace, but as something owed. ⁵ But to him who doesn't work, but believes in him who justifies the ungodly, his faith is accounted for righteousness."

The amazing thing is, when we submit to God, do not quench the Holy Spirit, and begin to live as He tells us, our actions become a reflection of Him, and others will witness the fruits of the spirit right before their eyes.

1 Corinthians 13:4-7

"Love is patient and is kind. Love doesn't envy. Love doesn't brag, is not proud, ⁵ doesn't behave itself inappropriately, doesn't seek its own way, is not provoked, takes no account of evil; ⁶ doesn't rejoice in unrighteousness, but rejoices with the truth; ⁷ bears all things, believes all things, hopes all things, and endures all things."

How beautiful is this? God took our burdens, placed them on Himself, and gave us a choice to accept these gifts (characteristics of His love we can express towards others) for all of us to live and thrive in. This is not to say that we will not face challenging times. The Bible does not promise that; in fact, it promises that we will experience trials and tribulation; however, we can still experience love, peace, and joy during these times through Jesus.

John 16:33

"I have told you these things, that in me you may have peace. In the world you have trouble; but cheer up! I have overcome the world."

James 1:12

"Blessed is a person who endures temptation, for when he has been approved, he will receive the crown of life which the Lord promised to those who love him."

Romans 8:18

"For I consider that the sufferings of this present time are not worthy to be compared with the glory which will be revealed toward us."

Grace is a gift for all who make the decision to trust in God. Jesus knows all that we have done and our true hearts. I would like to let you know that even if you have committed all the sins above, it is not too late for you to give your life to Jesus. The enemy is good at making us feel that we have strayed too far from God for Him to still love us. That it is too late to repent and receive new life in Christ and forgiveness. The suffering in silence ends today as we all join and build up one another through the love of God. You can repent today and confess your sins to Jesus Christ. No human will ever provide us with the grace and mercy God does. With a pure and humble heart, I implore you to say the following to our Savior.

Take A Step Closer to Jesus

Jesus, I come to you in full repentance of my sins and ask for your forgiveness. I believe You died for my sins and rose on the third day. I know that I cannot go through this life on my own. Please guide and correct me on my path, for my nature is to sin due to this fleshly body. Protect me from all evil; I trust in you, Lord. I invite you into my life, proclaiming you as God in the flesh, Lord, and Savior. Thank you for loving me as I am and wanting the best for me. In Jesus name, Amen.

I pray this has brought everyone comfort and knowing that God will leave the ninety-nine for the one. Never believe that God does not care for you in all seasons of your life.

My Burden to Bear has now become my proclamation for Jesus and I am truly blessed to have shared it with you!

END

Notes:

Chapter One- Getting to Know Jesus

1. Gubikian, G. (2011). *The Deity of Jesus Christ in the Old and New Testaments.* Xulon Press.

Chapter Two- The Gift of Grace

1. Bible Hub. (n.d.-a). Retrieved June 1, 2024, from https://biblehub.com/greek/4905.htm
2. Bible Hub. (n.d.-b). Retrieved June 1, 2024, from https://biblehub.com/greek/630.htm
3. Bible Hub. (n.d.-c). Retrieved June 1, 2024, from https://biblehub.com/hebrew/5959.htm
4. Bible Hub. (n.d.-d). Retrieved June 1, 2024, from https://biblehub.com/text/matthew/1-24.htm
5. Bible Hub. (n.d.-e). Retrieved June 1, 2024, from https://biblehub.com/text/matthew/1-25.htm
6. Bible Hub. (n.d.-f). Retrieved June 1, 2024, from https://biblehub.com/greek/3933.htm
7. Bible Hub. (n.d.-g). Retrieved June 1, 2024, from https://biblehub.com/greek/2532.htm
8. Bible Hub. (n.d.-h). Retrieved June 1, 2024, from https://biblehub.com/greek/1097.htm

9. Bible Hub. (n.d.-i). Retrieved June 1, 2024, from https://biblehub.com/greek/5487.htm
10. Bible Hub. (n.d.-j) Retrieved June 1, 2024, from https://biblehub.com/greek/5485.htm
11. Bible Hub. (n.d.-k). Retrieved June 1, 2024, from https://biblehub.com/text/luke/1-48.htm
12. Bible Hub. (n.d.-l). Retrieved June 1, 2024, from https://biblehub.com/greek/4815.htm
13. Bible Hub. (n.d.-m). Retrieved June 1, 2024, from https://biblehub.com/greek/5014.htm
14. Bible Hub. (n.d.-n). Retrieved June 1, 2024, from https://biblehub.com/greek/5013.htm
15. Freeman, J.M. (n.d.). *Manners and Customs of the Bible*. Bible Truth Publishers. October 19, 2024, Retrieved From https://bibletruthpublishers.com/manners-and-customs-of-the-bible/lbd23559
16. Chapter 18E-The Virgin Misconception Myth. (n.d.). Jews for Judaism. Retrieved October 24,2024, from https://jewsforjudaism.org/knowledge/articles/chapter-18e-virgin-misconception-myth

Chapter Three- Clarity and The Importance of Jesus's Way into the World.

1. Gubikian, G. (2011). *The Deity of Jesus Christ in the Old and New Testaments.* Xulon Press.
2. Bible Hub. (n.d.-n). Retrieved June 1, 2024, from https://biblehub.com/greek/5043.htm
3. Bible Hub. (n.d.-o). Retrieved June 1, 2024, from https://biblehub.com/greek/5207.htm
4. Strobel, L. (1998, 2016). *The Case for Christ: A Journalist's Personal Investigation of the Evidence for Jesus.* Grand Rapids, Zondervan.

ABOUT THE AUTHOR

Gabrielle is making her Christian Author debut with ***My Burden to Bear!*** Although this is her first published piece, the dedication, passion, and time that has been poured into this writing shows not only her resilience but also the genuine love she has for God, His word & His sons' and daughters. A few things she enjoys are ice cream, time with her family and particularly those moments when we are completely exhausted after a long day and find everything funny before calling it a night. She is compassionate and bold. This book asks some challenging questions that burst the door open and ignite meaningful conversations. You can join in on Instagram @MyBurdentoBear and on YouTube @https://www.youtube.com/@GabrielleTK26.

www.ingramcontent.com/pod-product-compliance
Lightning Source LLC
Chambersburg PA
CBHW032059150426
43194CB00006B/588